An Angel in
My Garden

Alda Ellis

HARVEST HOUSE PUBLISHERS
EUGENE, OREGON 97402

An Angel in My Garden
Copyright ©1997
by Harvest House Publishers
Eugene, Oregon 97402

Library of Congress Cataloging-in-Publication Data
Ellis, Alda,1952-
An angel in my garden / Alda Ellis.
p. cm.
ISBN 1-56507-522-6 (alk.paper)
1. Christian life—Anacdotes.
2. Ellis, Alda, 1952-   3. Angels. I. Title.
BV4617.E45 1997   96-42955
242—dc20   CIP

Design and production by
Left Coast Design, Portland, Oregon

Unless otherwise indicated,
Scripture quotations are from
the King James Version.

Scripture quotations marked NIV are from The Holy Bible,
New International Version R. Copyright © 1973, 1978, 1984
by the International Bible Society. Used by permission
of Zondervan Publishing House.

Printed in the United States of America.
97 98 99 00 01 02 03 04 05 06 / QK / 10 9 8 7 6 5 4 3 2

Dedicated to my family,
for their generous love and
support through the years

Mother and Daddy, thank you for your
love and devotion in all my days.

Thank you to my loving husband,
for understanding and loving me through
all the work until wee hours in the morning.

Thank you to his parents,
for loving and helping in caring
for our two boys.

Thank you, Samuel and Mason,
whose hearts I cherish.

Contents

Life is made up, not of great sacrifices or duties,
but of little things, in which smiles and kindness
and small obligations, given habitually,
are what win and preserve the heart.

SIR HUMPHREY DAVY

*I*t seems that some people make life a garden. Their presence warms, inspires—waters the dry rows in our lives, sprouts hope in barren places. I call these people angels, for their influence is profound and full of kindness. They nurture my growth. They save me from harsh weather, storms within and without, and keep me blooming and productive.

I share their stories here—of a grandmother whose steady care grew not only a beautiful garden but a far-reaching realm of love and welcome; of two boys working as one to gladden their mother's heart; of flowers that thrive despite weeds; and of a stranger in the street wearing wings.

Notice who might have been an angel, who might have made a garden in your life today—someone who shared generously, cared simply, or just extended a needed touch. But most importantly, open your eyes and heart, for you may have the opportunity to be an angel in someone's garden yourself.

Out in the highways and byways of life,
Many are weary and sad;
Carry the sunshine where darkness is rife,
Making the sorrowing glad …
Make me a blessing to someone today.

IRA B. WILSON

*The best portion of
a good man's life—
his little, nameless,
unremembered
acts of kindness
and love.*

WILLIAM WORDSWORTH

My Grandmother's Garden

When I was a little girl growing up in the city, visiting my grandmother's home in the country every summer was quite a treat. After a two-hour car ride we met a warm welcome in open arms and generous hugs. Sun tea and fresh-squeezed lemonade watered our thirst after the long drive.

It was during one of those blissful summers in which I spent time alone with my grandmother that I discovered how wonderful was her garden. Neatly planted just a few steps from the kitchen door, past the well, with thrift in

bloom cascading over its borders, stood a white picket fence taller than I. At the entrance, hearty zinnias in every color imaginable greeted me, their heads reaching for the sun.

I, too, reached for the sun, savoring summer's invita-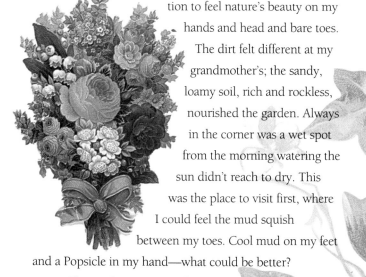tion to feel nature's beauty on my hands and head and bare toes. The dirt felt different at my grandmother's; the sandy, loamy soil, rich and rockless, nourished the garden. Always in the corner was a wet spot from the morning watering the sun didn't reach to dry. This was the place to visit first, where I could feel the mud squish between my toes. Cool mud on my feet and a Popsicle in my hand—what could be better?

The garden was more than a sensory delight to my grandmother. It was a creative means of feeding a family on a tight budget. It was a delightful and practical element in every year's living. Most of all, it was a reflection of Grandmother's greatest gift: her ability to warm and

nourish, in every season, all those who peopled her path. Grandmother's friendly spirit was a gift from the heart. Her bright "Hello!" "How are you?" and contagious smile flowed naturally from within. All those who passed her went away cheered. She and her garden drew strength from one another, and they shared it generously.

My grandmother had seen two world wars and a Depression. She bore four daughters and buried one. Yet through all the days of her life, one thing remained constant and unquestionably essential: her garden. Whether it provided money for shoes through an overabundant crop of tomatoes or just the pleasure of fresh black-eyed peas for dinner, the garden seemed one of life's basic necessities. In the same way, Grandmother weathered each storm with the same tenacity. She bloomed not just annually, but perennially.

Her angel's face
As the great eye of heaven shined bright,
And made a sunshine in the shady place;
Did never mortal eye behold such heavenly grace.

EDMUND SPENSER

I remember one weekend visit in which we found my grandmother using the garden for yet another need: a simple task in the face of deep worry. After the customary warm hugs, we saw tears. Grandmother fear-lessly hoed the dozen or so weeds that dared to spring up as she explained that Grandfather was not feeling well—he was having another "spell" with his heart. He rested inside as

she sought calm keeping busy in the garden. When the weeds were gone and the vegetables picked, it was the worry she worked at with the hoe.

After my grandfather died, the garden became even more my grandmother's place of loving labor and gentle solace. She spent winter months deciding what variety of tomato to plant next year. Seed catalogues filled a basket

next to her chair and kept her gardening wisdom up to date. Summer months saw the usual blooms, blossoms, and rich produce. Zinnias still greeted visitors, as they reseeded themselves year after year. Grandmother hoed away not worry but loneliness, and passersby acknowledged the rewards: "What a beautiful garden you have!" Sweet corn filled a freezer. Tomatoes went to friends at church. Zinnias decorated the altar.

It was a particularly hot summer when my grandmother became ill. On another weekend visit we found her in the garden as usual, smiling amidst a profusion of pea vines. Hugs were full yet fragile. The garden bloomed with all its summer strength, yet Grandmother

laid her hoe against the picket fence with a weary hand.
Words were not needed for what lay ahead.

In the years since I have taken my sons to visit the
place where I tasted love and beauty so consistently. A
family lives there now and much has changed. Bicycles
dot the front lawn and a favorite
apple tree is gone. The
old picket fence
stands in need of
paint around the
area where
Grandmother's
garden thrived. I
leave it with not
sadness but a
smile, as a few red
zinnias catch my eye.

Few people have the
gift of spirit that Grandmother
had. You may be one of them.
Whose life can you gladden
today?

To love for the sake of being loved is human,
but to love for the sake of loving is angelic.

ALPHONSE DE LAMARTINE

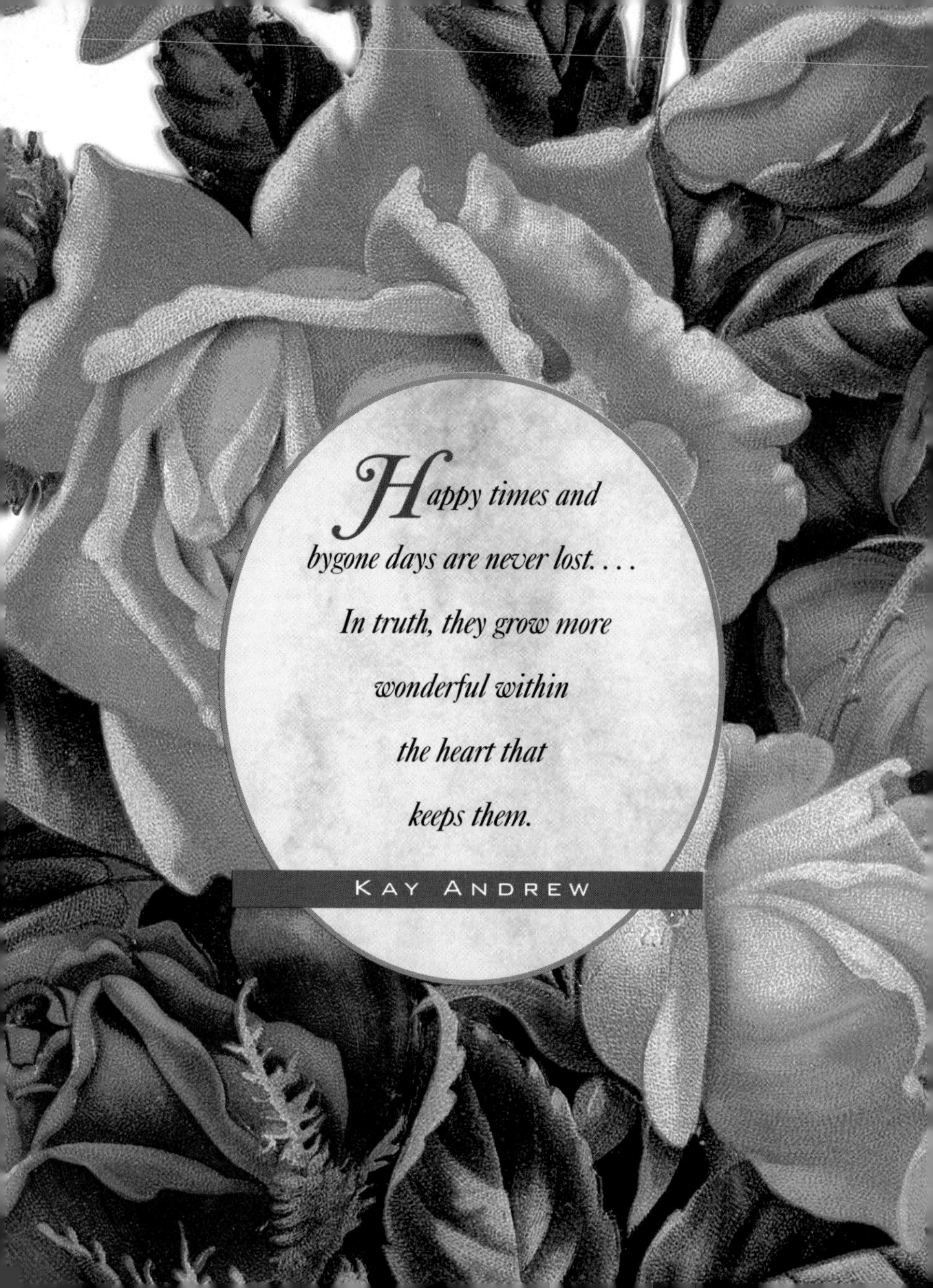

*H*appy times and
bygone days are never lost. . . .
In truth, they grow more

wonderful within

the heart that

keeps them.

KAY ANDREW

Roots of Love

We sat in the front porch swing, my husband and I, remembering my parents' fiftieth wedding anniversary party. After a year's careful planning, we all experienced a lovely journey in time as we watched two loved and loving people celebrate five decades of faithfulness and joy. We recalled the glorious Sunday afternoon during which more than two hundred friends and relatives came to offer congratulations. Some of the friendships stretched even beyond the fifty years we honored.

The porch swing creaked as we swung gently through the memories. As we reminisced, a sudden summer shower descended. We were amused watching our two little boys playing. We sipped

> *Let love and faithfulness never leave you; bind them around your neck, write them on the tablet of your heart.*
>
> **PROVERBS 3:3** NIV

iced tea; they, with heads tilted back and mouths open, drank the rain. At that moment, watching these young versions of the next generation, I realized something: We had given my parents a party, but they had given us something more important that day. They had given us an example of unwavering devotion.

They had given us roots in a garden of abundance.

These children truly came from a long line of love. Their other grandparents and great-grandparents had also celebrated golden anniversaries. Generations had lived and loved long, weaving deep roots. Faithfulness was their legacy to our boys. These white-haired angels had cultivated a grand garden.

As the shower passed, our boys were soaked. The

sun peeked out. As we left the swing to join the boys, we saw a common miracle—a brilliant rainbow arched through the sky. We stood still for a moment, savoring. Mason, the oldest, watched quietly but five-year-old Samuel's interest faded quickly, drawn by the sight of a delicately beautiful butterfly. The rose the butterfly chose for landing was dotted with raindrops; it seemed he stopped for a cool drink much as we had moments before. A little hand reached to catch him but was not as quick, and the butterfly hastily winged his way to other, safer flowers.

The butterfly finished my lesson for the day. As I watched it I uncovered a deeper truth. Yes, our boys had witnessed the culmination of decades of love, but it was up to us as parents to sow, water, and protect the precious seeds they had inherited. And then, when their roots were strong, we were to give them wings.

Youth's the season made for joys,
Love is then our duty.

ROBERT GAY

It's just the little homely things,

The unobtrusive friendly things,

The "won't you let me help you" things

that make our pathway light.

GRACE HAINOS

Simplest
of Pleasures

My favorite season of the year is autumn. The summer's heat is passed and the trees put on a show of spectacular color. Walking down the hill, with two little boys' hands in mine, we go to check on the gourds we planted last spring.

It all began with a handful of seeds, deposited thoughtfully in the season's receptive soil. It seems natural to little boys' nature to dig in the dirt, so I gave my sons some seeds to make their digging productive. They then deliberated where the planting should take place. It had to

be out of the way of Dad's tractor so that when
seeds sprouted, they wouldn't be mowed. They
couldn't be placed under the hundred-year-old oak
tree that stood guard over the pasture, for its branches
provided shade, not sun. Finally a special place
presented itself: The path favored by the
dogs, who chased anything that hopped,
was just perfect. The site lay untouched by
anything other than animal tracks and
each year's crop of leaves.

The two little boys were so busy
planting their seeds, they didn't even
see me standing nearby, enjoying their
work. Today they were the angels of my
garden. What a joy for a mother to behold:
two brothers working in harmony toward the same goal—
agreeing with each other, helping each other. Today, too, I
saw reborn a long line of land-lovers, people who nourished
the land and were in turn nourished by it . . . people who
savored the soft bed and rich scent of earth, who invested in
it and cared for it. It was a family tradition celebrated today
by little hands and hopeful hearts. I silently said a prayer
that the other seeds my boys sow, in their own gardens of
life, will be ones of kindness.

24

That sweet, hot summer day passed and others followed, and the time came to gather the boys for a trek to the pasture to see what had developed. Breaking loose of my hands, they started running, for shining up ahead was a golden heap of treasures. Trying not to step on the vines sprawling the ground, each boy selected ripe gourds and placed them in my basket. Returning to the house was an effort in itself because the basket was overflowing with playful gourds that kept jumping out of the basket to roll down the gentle slope of our hill.

Once all boys and gourds were accounted for, we sat on the back-door steps with a sigh of relief and admired the plunder. Samuel shared with me his secret in gleaning such a magnificent harvest. He planted not one but three seeds in each hole, "so God would be sure and see them."

Sitting on the steps, I am quietly grateful watching my sons glory in their prizes. Whether it's checking the growth of yellow gourds or chatty boys, the simplest of pleasures are right here at my back door.

Simple pleasures help us see
Just how lovely life can be.

*T*here are persons so radiant,

so genial, so kind, so pleasure-

bearing, that you instinctively feel in

their presence that they do you good,

whose coming into a room is like

the bringing of a lamp there.

HENRY WARD BEECHER

The Seeds
We've Planted

Gardeners or not, we're all planters of seeds. The seeds may be good, full of kindness and courage, or they may be bad and drain health and vitality. In my little home church, through the years I've seen the planting and harvest of thousands of good seeds, all sown by folks who gave without expectation of return. It was there I learned that a good gardener—or angel—never measures her giving, never waits for thanks. She scatters her seeds as far, and as deep and as often, as she can.

Ours is a charming little rock church with three

stained glass windows. Ivy covers some of its walls and moss carpets the stone walkway. My mother and daddy helped to build this church. Little did they know they were also "constructing" a garden—one that was full of angels.

Daddy was one of them; he made small repairs and taught the men's Bible class. Mother served as "the music lady," traveling from class to class on Sunday mornings to teach the children songs. Another musical angel, Mrs. Hill, shone especially on Easter when with her wonderful voice she moved us with soaring solos.

The Christmas season brought out another of our garden's gifts. Mrs. Lindsay, an art teacher, spent a whole year painting a larger-than-life manger scene. Her skillful strokes created in painstaking detail Mary, Joseph, an angel, shepherds, wise men, camels, donkeys, sheep, and baby Jesus. The first Saturday in December, for as long as I can remember, the men of the church collected their tools and erected each character. The angel was hung in a tree to oversee the manger, and a spotlight was adjusted just so to highlight its pleasure.

In my girlhood we passed this scene coming home

from Christmas-shopping. Busy traffic actually slowed to study this poignant reminder of the season's real center. It seemed to add to the excitement in the air as we strolled from the bus stop to our house two blocks away, our arms filled with packages.

Mrs. Lindsay's efforts touched many besides that first congregation. Her Nativity figures became part of our community's annual decorations. Children who saw the scene built

> *Make a rule, and pray God to help you keep it, never, if possible, to lie down at night without being able to say, "I have made one human being, at least, a little wiser, a little happier, or a little better this day."*
>
> **CHARLES KINGSLEY**

years ago now help erect it for the next generation to enjoy.

Christmas Eve, the Nativity scene played a central role in our celebration. Each church member, holding a candle, filed out of the sanctuary, the awe of the setting silencing us. We circled the scene, faces glowing, and sang "Silent Night." We paused for a moment before blowing out our candles and gazed at the stars just as the wise men and shepherds did centuries ago. I closed my eyes and tried to imagine the manger. . . . Then piercing the winter wind

were church bells, ringing loudly. Everyone received generous doses of hugs and glad tidings before we scurried home in the chill, holding Christmas in our hearts.

Years passed, and our church "garden" remained fruitful, dotted with angels to make burdens light. My best friend's brother, once seen as a relentless pest, became my loving husband. We married in the church of my childhood. Mrs. Hill sang in the choir that day. A few years later, my Sunday school class planned a baby shower for us. The baby had his own schedule, however, and arrived early. My husband displayed his good nature by playing the honoree at the shower, corsage and all. Both of our sons were christened at the church.

Women's groups gathered regularly, then and now, to make quilts for youth homes or to create loving packages for the prison. These angels of all ages respond quickly to give, knowing there's always someone who needs to receive.

Board meetings, potluck dinners complete with Mrs. Esco's turkey and dressing, bazaars, and holiday festivities made up the church traditions we carry on today. My mother is still "the music lady."

Daddy still fixes locks and repairs leaks.

Last Sunday, on the occasion of the church's fiftieth anniversary, my twelve-year-old stood to tell what the little rock building meant to him. Mrs. Hill was in the choir. My parents watched proudly and my husband patted my shoulder, for I had a terrible lump in my throat. My son spoke of how the church was a garden with seeds carefully planted, flowers blooming with good deeds everywhere. The flowers were the people he loved—Mrs. May, who hugged him every week, his Sunday school teacher, and ninety-two-year-old Mrs. Esco (and her turkey).

"God sees the seeds we've planted," he said—*and the harvest that's come from them*, I thought. "If we could, we'd see God smile."

*May you reap a harvest of blessing
from the seeds of kindness you have sown.*

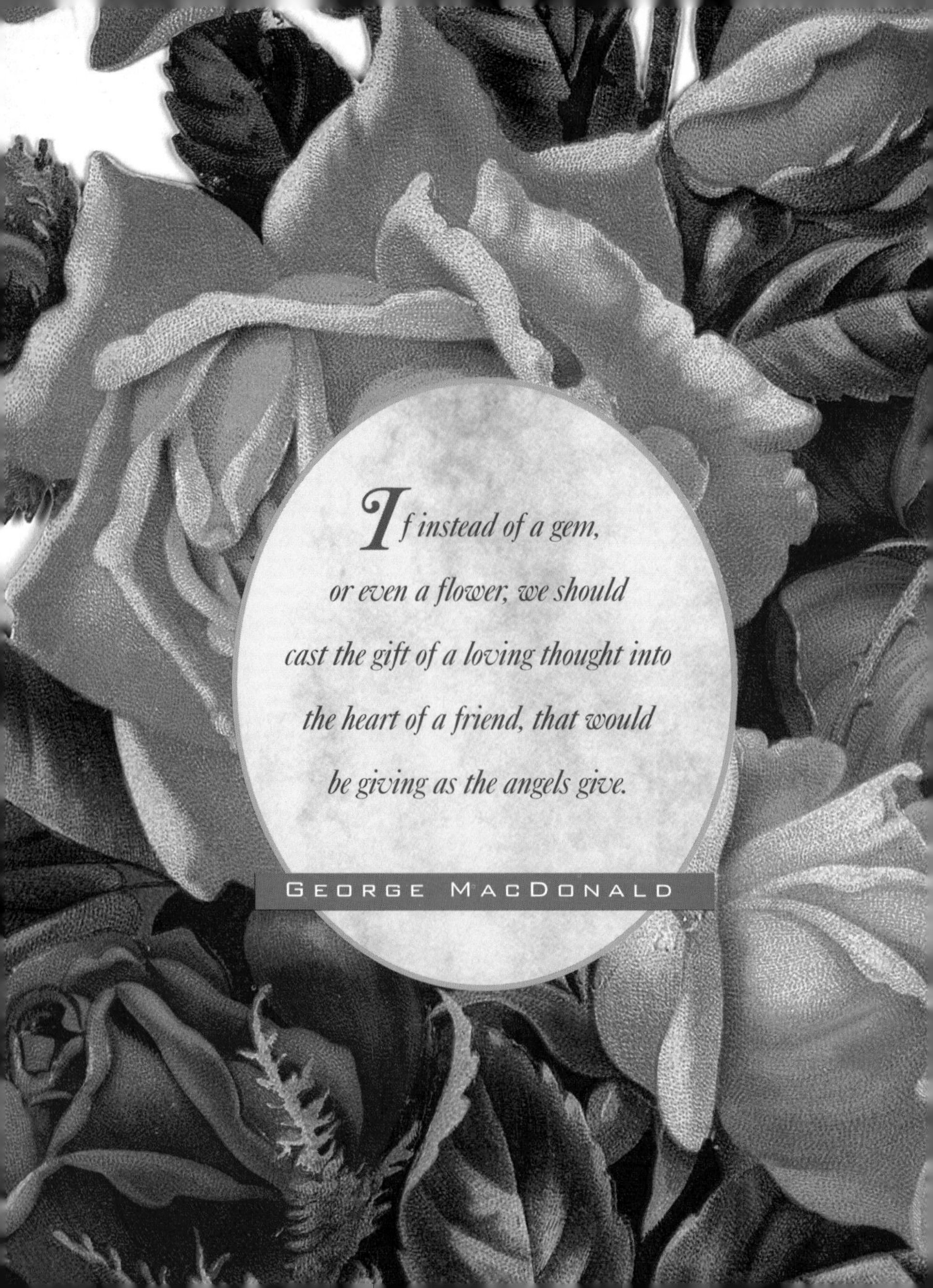

If instead of a gem,

or even a flower, we should

cast the gift of a loving thought into

the heart of a friend, that would

be giving as the angels give.

GEORGE MACDONALD

Weeds in My Garden

*L*ast fall I decided to plant more tulip bulbs in my garden. On my knees, digging up the rocky soil, I savored planting the thirty-six bulbs one by one. The sunshine warmed my back, grass stains dirtied my knees, and a cool, crisp breeze rushed across my sweaty face. I pulled off my dirty gloves as I wiped my brow and sat on a nearby stone to sip a glass of iced tea. My thoughts went back to the day I was dealt a dose of weeds along with my flowers.

It seemed a short time ago that on a routine visit to my doctor, he found a problem he felt required more testing. Needless to say, waking from surgery and hearing that I had cancer was a shock in itself, because I never even considered the possibility. Thinking of my small sons, I immediately asked God for guidance.

It seems God brings us to our knees when we least expect it. Lying in a hospital bed proved humbling for me. I felt I was at the mercy of others, unable to do anything for myself. My self-confidence gave way to fearful glances at my future. My faith drew me closer to God because I needed Him so much.

Even amongst weeds, though, a garden can grow, and angels can guide people through it. One of my richest gifts was my husband's constant devotion. While I recovered emotionally and physically, he stood by. He kept the house running, making sure the boys caught the school bus, had lunches, and wore clean clothes. He lifted my spirits, telling me confidently and quietly that all would be well again soon. I never had to ask for anything; he knew instinctively what I needed and brought it. He nurtured my weakened body and heart back to strength.

Friends and relatives overwhelmed me with thoughtful words and deeds. Flowers, cards, and visits for me, and meals for my family, all bespoke a love deep and wide. We arrived home to find the lawn mowed or groceries provided, again without our asking. If someone saw a need, he or she met it without taking credit or needing thanks.

> *Our hearts are like a garden spot*
> *Where only Friends may sow*
> *Here thorns and thistles flourish not*
> *But Friendship's flowers grow.*
>
> **1901 GREETING CARD**

In the three years since, roses smell a little sweeter, I laugh a little louder and hug a little tighter. And I plant more flowers. It is with faith that I plant these bulbs in the fall, in hope of seeing their beauty in the spring. My faith says God will bring those bulbs to bloom even though I might not be here to see them.

There are so many flower beds left to tend at my

house. There are two boys to raise, others to teach in Sunday school, homeless people to feed, goals to sponsor, charities to support. In short, there are many people to love, knowing that we may never cross paths again. There are lives that can be changed because of one tiny seed of kindness that I plant, much as my dear ones did when I was in the hospital. Even though I may never see the fruits of my labor, faith carries me through the good times and the bad. My faith assures me, there *will* be fruit.

Weeds will always interfere with my planting. Will I see those or the flowers? It's all in how I tend my garden.

Do all the good you can
By all the means you can,
In all the ways you can,
In all the places you can,
At all the times you can,
To all the people you can,
As long as ever you can.

JOHN WESLEY

I expect to pass through
this world but once; any good
thing therefore that I can do,
or any kindness that I can
show to any fellow-creature,
let me do it now. . . .

STEPHEN GRELLET

A Rose in the City

A visit to the City always leaves me longing for the soothing stillness of my garden. Times Square hustles and bustles at a never-ending pace. Billboards shout their messages to those below. Horns blare from the yellow ribbon of taxis that lines the streets. Subway steam shoots through gutters while cold jabs those who venture onto the streets. Yet angels can inhabit such a place.

On a visit recently we and some friends walked the

blocks from our hotel to an Italian eatery.
Lingering over dinner was a pleasure,
for the food was delicious. We had a
sizable serving left when we had
finished, and though the waiter
packaged it for us to take home, we knew it
wouldn't last in the hotel. I wondered if I could share
it with someone now, while it was still warm. To whom
could I be an angel this night?

I had seen many homeless wandering the streets
earlier, but now I could find no one with whom to share
this wonderful dinner. Storefront after storefront was
empty of the faces I was looking for. As we drew closer to
our hotel I grew disappointed. The dinner would soon be
cold, and wasted, if I didn't hurry. I clutched the brown
paper bag tightly as I searched from street to street for
someone in need of a gift.

It was then that I felt a light tug on my arm.
Where she came from, I will never know. But she was
the woman I had been looking for. She told me she was
hungry. Her dark eyes were dim with weariness. A scarf
neatly covered her hair. But it was her hands that haunt

me. They were bound in rags to keep them from the cold.
Swollen and knobby fingers reached for the warm meal.
I gave it gladly, remembering that our circumstances
meant little in such a case: We were much more alike
than different. We were two women in the heart of a city,
looking to one another for aid.

After exchanging names, we said good-bye to the
woman as she moved down the street. Away she

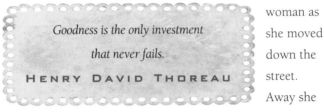

*Goodness is the only investment
that never fails.*

HENRY DAVID THOREAU

swept into the darkness split here and there by neon
lights. Somehow I was a little warmer walking home for
having met her. What she did not know was
that she fed me, too. She reminded me of a
path I might be walking. She reminded me
that gratitude should be my native language.
She showed me the picture of a life void of
all but the ability to receive and
with what grace one can do so.
What I had done seemed so

small, but isn't that what love is all about? A simple caring and sharing. When you have what someone needs, you offer it, and they to you. I needed to give, the street woman to receive. We helped each other.

And another angel appeared, right in the heart of the "concrete jungle." And the street woman whose name was Rose will always be my angel on the sidewalks of New York City.

Who in your garden hungers today—for a meal, for a hug, for a friendly face? To whom can you be an angel today?

I am to bless the world through what I am.

WILLIAM MAKEPEACE THACKERY

Every act of kindness
Moves to a larger one
Till friendships bloom to show
What little deeds have done.

JUNE MASTERS BACHER

Through these stories I have shown you the angels in my gardens. As you reflect on them, my desire is for you to find the angels in your garden, to feel the brush of wings, to see the celestial in the simplest of acts.

Even more, I hope you will be an angel wherever you can. Cultivate your own gardens. Let the power of small tasks performed without measure flow through your hands as life-giving seeds. You, too, will have fruit to harvest.